BLUES BANJO

BY FRED SOKOLOW

The Recording

Banjo and Vocals: Fred Sokolow
Sound Engineer: Michael Monagan
Recorded and Mixed at Sossity Sound

Editorial assistance by Ronny S. Schiff
Cover photos by Lynn Shipley Sokolow

To access audio visit:
www.halleonard.com/mylibrary

Enter Code
5547-7914-7366-0478

ISBN 978-1-4803-2861-7

HAL•LEONARD®
CORPORATION

7777 W. BLUEMOUND RD. P.O. BOX 13819 MILWAUKEE, WI 53213

In Australia Contact:
Hal Leonard Australia Pty. Ltd.
4 Lentara Court
Cheltenham, Victoria, 3192 Australia
Email: ausadmin@halleonard.com.au

Visit Hal Leonard Online at
www.halleonard.com

CONTENTS

INTRODUCTION

Blues on a banjo? It's not such an anomaly, when you consider that African slaves brought the banjo to America, and they probably brought the blues, as well. We only have recordings of a few early 20th century banjo-playing bluesmen (Papa Charlie Jackson, Gus Cannon), but long before recording technology existed, the first blues songs played in this country may well have been played on banjos. Guitars were too expensive for working folks until the end of the 19th century, when the Sears catalog offered several inexpensive gut-string models for a few dollars each. Until then, if you could afford to buy a guitar, you were probably too wealthy to sing the down-and-out blues!

Besides, blues sounds great on a banjo, as you'll hear when you listen to the audio that accompanies this book. However, this is not just a collection of songs. The blues tunes in this book will show you how to accompany or solo on any blues song and ad lib in a blues vein, whether you play alone or with other musicians. You'll be introduced to the styles and blues nuances of the great blues players. You'll get all the scales, licks, chords, and theory you need to improvise blues solos in any key, all over the fretboard. All the tab-and-music samples (songs, exercises, etc.) are played on the accompanying audio tracks, so you can hear the rhythmic timing of each tune and each lick. Using traditional banjo tunings, you'll find yourself playing blues licks you thought were only possible on guitar.

So grab your banjo and get started. Whatever kind of music you like to play, occasionally you'll need to put some blues in it. And remember: the best way to lose the blues is to play the blues!

Good luck,

Fred Sokolow

Fred Sokolow

ABOUT THE AUDIO

To access the audio examples that accompany this book, simply go to **www.halleonard.com/mylibrary** and enter the code found on page 1. The examples that include audio are marked with an icon throughout the book. This includes all the licks, tunes, and exercises that are written out in music and tablature. It's always helpful to listen to each musical track several times before trying to play the written music/tablature.

ABOUT THE BLUES—SOME BASICS

If you listen to contemporary and retro blues recordings, you'll be surprised by the variety of sounds identified as "the blues." If you don't believe it, listen to Bessie Smith, Charles Brown, Robert Johnson, Mississippi John Hurt, B.B. King, Reverend Gary Davis, Blind Blake, Muddy Waters, Memphis Minnie, Lightning Hopkins, Elmore James, Skip James, and Eric Clapton, just for a start. There's slick, urban jazzy blues, down-and-out bottleneck guitar blues, fancy fingerpicking raggy blues, and screaming electric blues/rock.

Despite all the variety, many (not all) blues songs share certain musical features...

THREE CHORDS (CHORD FAMILIES)

There's an old gag about the difference between a blues player and a jazz player: the blues player plays three chords for a thousand people, and the jazz player plays a thousand chords for three people. The truth is, thousands of blues songs *can* be played with three chords — the 1, 4, and 5 chords (often represented by the Roman numerals I, IV, and V). Those are the three chords whose *roots* (the note that names them) are the first, fourth, and fifth notes in the major scale of the key in which you're playing. The first, fourth, and fifth notes in the C major scale are C, F, and G, so a three-chord blues in C consists of C, F, and G (or C7, F7, and G7; seventh chords are often used in the blues, instead of major chords). In any key, the 1, 4, and 5 chords are called a *chord family*.

12-BAR BLUES

A *bar* is a unit of time. When you hear a drummer start a tune by clicking his sticks together over his head and shouting "One, two, three, four," he's counting out one bar of 4/4 time, a typical, four-beats-to-the-bar blues tempo.

Most pop music is divided into 8- or 16-bar phrases, so the *12-bar* format is unique to the blues. Several of the tunes in this book are 12-bar songs; it's the stereotypical blues format.

A 12-bar tune is made of three phrases. Each phrase is four bars long:

- The *first phrase* is four bars of the 1 chord. (One common variation: sometimes the second bar is a 4 chord.)

- The *second phrase* is two bars of 4, then two bars of 1. Often, the lyric of the first phrase is repeated.

- The *third phrase* is two bars of 5, then two bars of 1. It's the "answering phrase" that, lyrically and musically, completes the statement that was made and repeated in the first two phrases. Sometimes the second bar is 4, instead of 5. Often, the last two bars consist of a "turnaround" (see following section).

TURNAROUNDS

The *turnaround* is a two-bar phrase that ends a 12- or 8-bar blues. The turnaround usually ends on a 5 chord, and musically "sets up" the next verse. There are several different turnarounds in this book. A turnaround also makes a good musical introduction to a tune; you can play an instrumental version of the last two or four bars of the progression, or play an instrumental version of the turnaround.

Note: The tunes and licks in this chapter are played in G tuning. From fifth to first string, that's gDGBD.

TURNAROUNDS IN G

12-BAR BLUES IN G

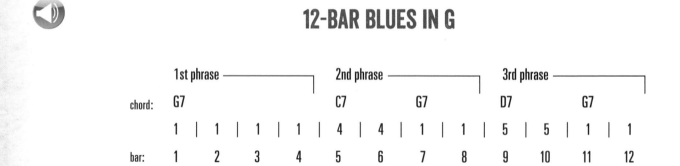

You can play the above 12-bar progression to backup many famous blues and rock songs, such as "Stormy Monday," "Every Day I Have the Blues," "(Going to) Kansas City," "Route 66," "Johnny B. Goode," "Whole Lotta Shakin' Goin' On," "Hound Dog," "Dust My Broom," "Shake, Rattle, and Roll," and, as in the recorded example, "See See Rider." To play along with the example, strum four downstrokes for each bar, with an upstroke after the third strum:

STRUM PATTERN

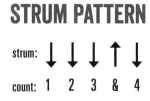

8-BAR BLUES

The 8-bar blues format is not as prevalent as the 12-bar progression, but there are many popular 8-bar blues tunes, including "How Long, How Long Blues," "Sitting on Top of the World," "You Got to Move," "Come Back Baby," "It Hurts Me Too," "The Night Life," and "Key to the Highway."

G7		C7		G7	D7	G7	D7
1	1	4	4	1	5	1	5

Sometimes the second bar is a 5 chord, and there are many turnaround possibilities for the last two bars.

A BASIC BOOGIE BACKUP LICK

The banjo accompaniment in the next example consists of a very popular boogie backup lick that is moveable. It's based on a barred chord that can be played up and down the fretboard. This boogie lick became a standard rock guitar backup (think of Chuck Berry's typical accompaniment lick on the bass strings), but it goes back as far as the 1930s Mississippi Delta blues recordings. You can hear Robert Johnson playing it in tunes like "I Believe I'll Dust My Broom." Here's the lick and some rhythmic and harmonic variations:

BOOGIE BACKUP VARIATIONS

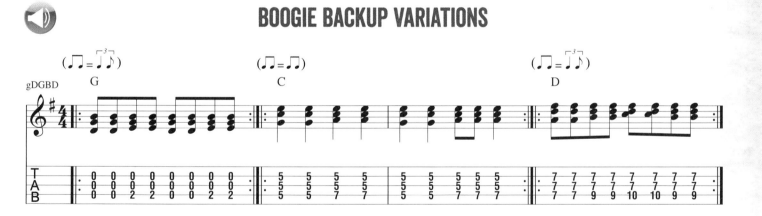

The 8-bar blues "Never Miss the Water," below, illustrates the use of the boogie backup lick.

"NEVER MISS THE WATER"

PLAYING THE BLUES IN G TUNING

G tuning is perhaps the most popular tuning for 5-string banjo today, partly because it's the standard tuning for bluegrass players. From fifth string to first string it's: gDGBD. This resembles the four highest strings of the "open G" Delta blues guitar tuning that many blues legends used. Therefore, many classic blues licks can be duplicated on the banjo in G tuning.

In the late 1920s, companies like Victor and Columbia began recording solo blues guitarists of the rural South. Some of the rawest, most soulful playing came out of the Mississippi Delta region. The resulting recordings of Charley Patton, Son House, Robert Johnson, and their peers became the foundation of modern blues. Early electric blues giants of the 1950s, like Muddy Waters and Howlin' Wolf, who defined the urban, electric blues sound, grew up listening to these Delta bluesmen, sometimes jamming with them, and their music was profoundly influenced by them.

"Fourteen Years," on the next page, is a 12-bar tune in the 1930s Delta blues style of Son House and Robert Johnson, not unlike "Walkin' Blues" or "Death Letter Blues." Like many blues tunes, it uses seventh chords and the melody is built on the G minor pentatonic scale.

SEVENTH CHORDS IN G TUNING

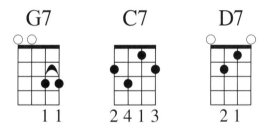

Here's the G minor pentatonic scale. Repeat it over and over as written to become familiar with it. The solos that follow, in the key of G, are built mostly from these notes:

G MINOR PENTATONIC SCALE (FIRST POSITION)

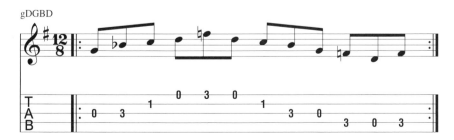

CHOKING

There are some "choked" notes in the next solo, and in most blues solos. A *choke* means raising the pitch of a note by stretching the string with the fretting finger, after picking it (also called "bending"). Choke the lower-pitched strings (the fourth and third) by pulling down, toward the floor, and choke the higher-pitched strings (the second and first) by raising them up, toward the ceiling. Here's how a choked string looks in tablature, and how it sounds:

CHOKING A STRING

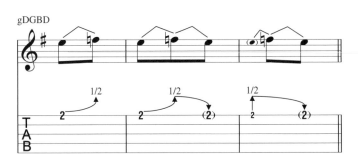

"FOURTEEN YEARS" (BACKUP AND SOLO)

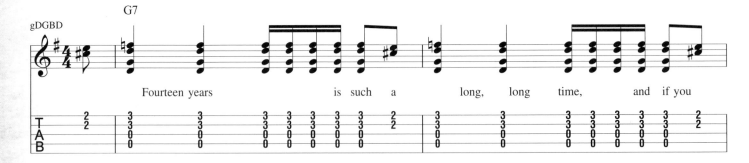

Fourteen years   is   such   a   long,   long   time,   and if you

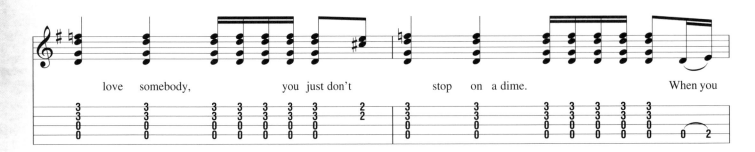

love   somebody,   you just don't   stop   on a dime.   When you

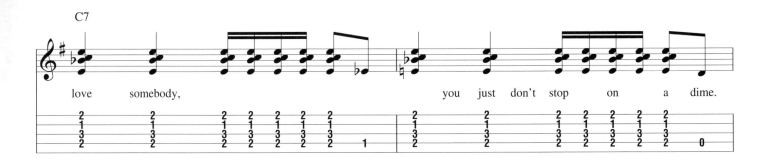

love   somebody,   you   just don't stop   on   a   dime.

Here's another way to play "Fourteen Years," with a shuffle beat feel, rather than the straight-eighths, rock rhythm of the previous version. This time around, you'll use some up-the-neck, barred chords for C and D:

BARRE CHORDS IN G TUNING

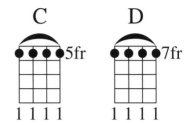

You can reach up three frets above a barred chord with your 4th finger (pinky), and get a seventh chord lick that you'll hear in the next version of "Fourteen Years." Son House used this technique in "Special Rider Blues," and you can hear it in Robert Johnson's "Cross Road Blues" and "Milkcow's Calf Blues."

C7 LICK

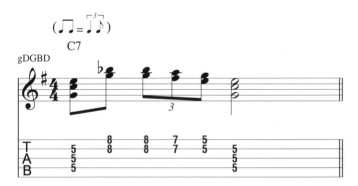

"FOURTEEN YEARS" (BARRE CHORDS)

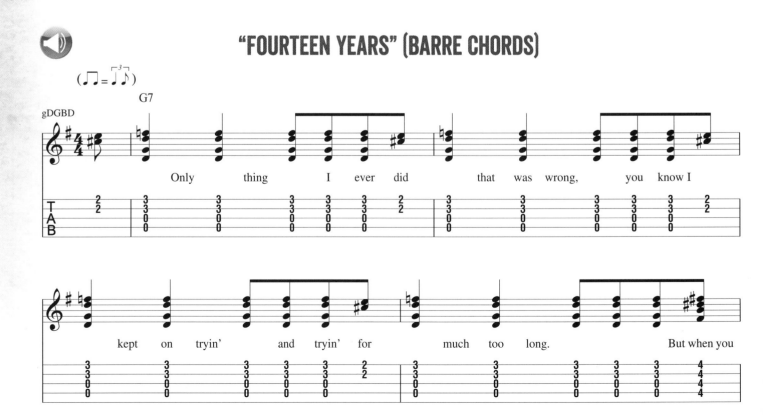

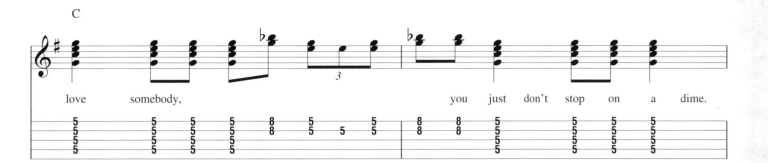

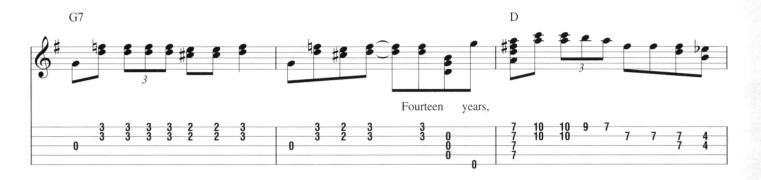

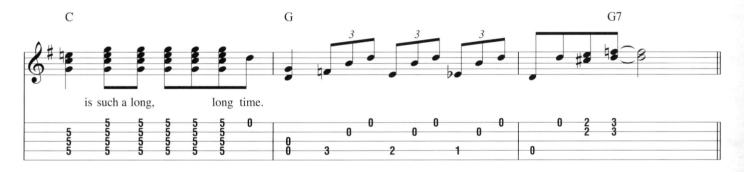

Many Delta blues tunes have a defining *riff*, a repeated musical phrase that is played throughout the tune, often during pauses in the singing. "Woke Up This Mornin'" is a good example. The tune is in the 12-bar form—roughly; there are some extra bars, due to the repetition of the tune's signature riff. It resembles "Rollin' and Tumblin' Blues," which was played by many Delta players ("Hambone" Willie Newbern, Muddy Waters). Robert Johnson's "If I Had Possession Over Judgement Day" is in a similar vein. In typical early 1930s blues style, you play the melody while singing it. For an instrumental break, you stop singing and your "accompaniment" becomes your solo.

"WOKE UP THIS MORNIN'"

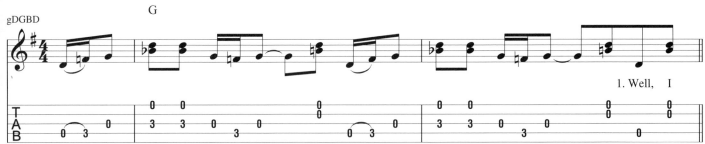

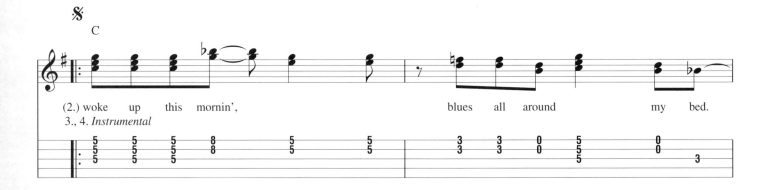

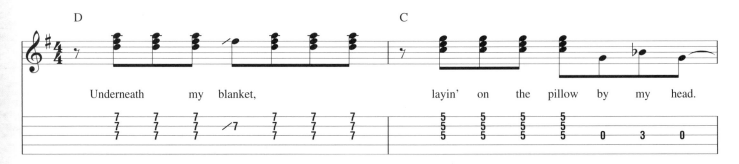

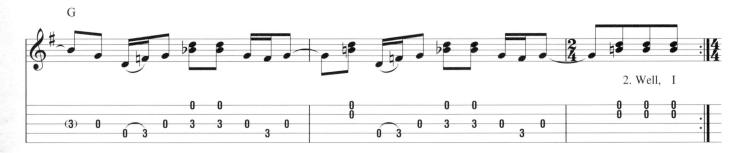

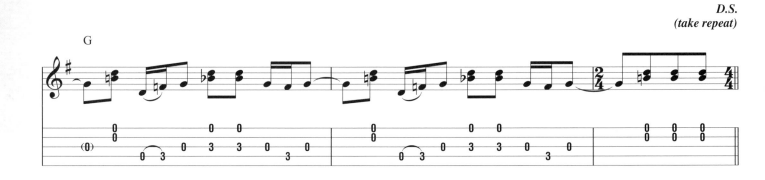

"So Long" is a slow 12-bar blues that resembles many Chicago-style electric blues standards, such as "Blues with a Feeling" (Little Walter) or Muddy Waters' "Honey Bee." It shows how to accompany a slow blues with up-the-neck chords like these:

UP-THE-NECK CHORDS

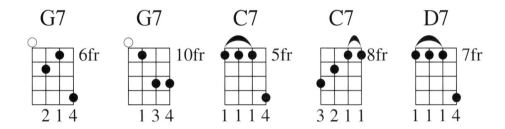

The use of these up-the-neck chords for vocal accompaniment goes back to the Delta. Listen to Robert Johnson's guitar backup as he sings "Malted Milk" or "Kindhearted Woman Blues."

"So Long," on the next page, begins with a typical intro: it's a brief solo over the last four bars of the 12-bar pattern, starting on the 5 chord (D7). Notice how the G♭7 in the second bar of the vocal part of the tune substitutes for the 4 chord (C). It's a common blues substitution. The opening lick, at the 11th and 12th frets, resembles the "train whistle" lick used by so many acoustic blues guitarists. Listen to Muddy Waters' intro to "Honey Bee" for an example.

"SO LONG" (BACKUP)

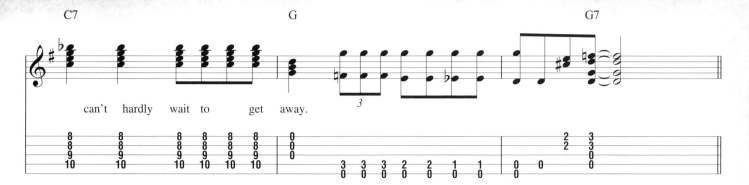

Here's an ad lib solo to "So Long," based on the first position G minor pentatonic scale. Play it and then ad lib your own solo, making up licks from the notes in the G minor pentatonic scale. Notice that the licks built on this scale work for all three chords (G, C, and D7).

"SO LONG" (SOLO)

A MOVEABLE BLUES BOX

In the late 1940s, T-Bone Walker and other blues guitarists switched from acoustic to electric guitar. The volume they gained enabled them to lead a swing band with horns, piano, drums, etc., and play guitar solos that could be heard above the din. They developed a single-note style of playing that involved moveable chord and scale positions, and played horn-like solos up and down the fretboard. The modern style of electric blues was born, with T-Bone (of "Stormy Monday" fame) as the midwife.

The blues scale below (sometimes called a *blues box*) is one of the moveable scales that makes this type of playing possible on banjo, guitar, or any instrument. It is a slight variation of the minor pentatonic scale and is based on the F formation. You don't have to fret the F formation constantly; it's a frame of reference. An F formation played at the 3rd, 4th, and 5th fret is a G chord, so the scale below is a G blues box:

G BLUES BOX

You can ad lib B.B. King-style, single-note licks using this blues position. This is a useful soloing technique when someone else (a guitar or any chording instrument) is playing chords. The solo to "Shuffle Blues" that follows is based on it. Once again, learn the solo and use the backup track to make up similar solos.

SHUFFLE BLUES (IN G)

Since this blues box is moveable (includes no open strings), you can use it to play single-note solos in any key. The licks based on it are moveable as well, so it's no harder to play in A♭ or E♭ than to play in G. Fret the F formation in the appropriate place to match the 1 chord, and you're good to go! For example, the version of "Shuffle Blues" that follows is in B♭. To get your left hand set for soloing, fret the F formation at the 6th, 7th, and 8th frets, where it's a B♭ chord.

SHUFFLE BLUES (IN B♭)

CHUCK BERRY-STYLE DOUBLE-NOTE LICKS

Using the F-formation-based moveable blues box, you can play double-note licks reminiscent of Chuck Berry and other early R&B guitarists. Following are some of the two-note licks, followed by a third version of "Shuffle Blues." This time it's in the key of C, based on the F formation at the 8th, 9th, and 10th frets. Playing the three versions of "Shuffle Blues," you can see how Chuck Berry's style grew out of T-Bone Walker's sound—and Berry has said so himself.

LICKS (KEY OF C)

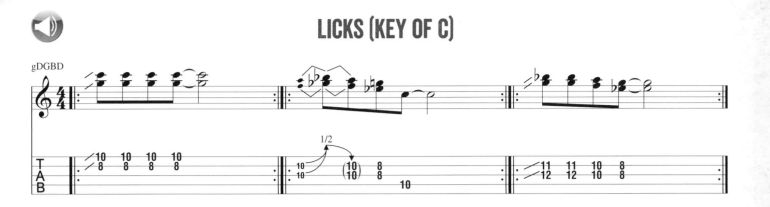

SHUFFLE BLUES (IN C WITH DOUBLE-NOTE LICKS)

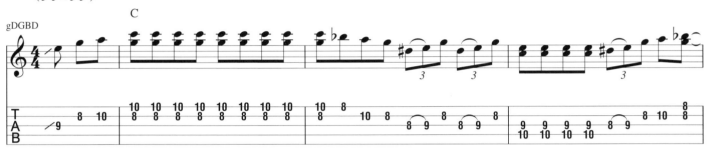

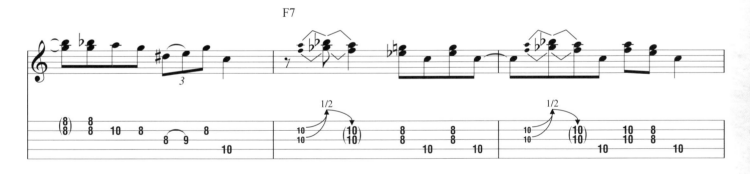

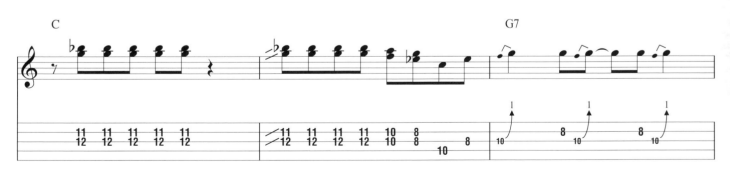

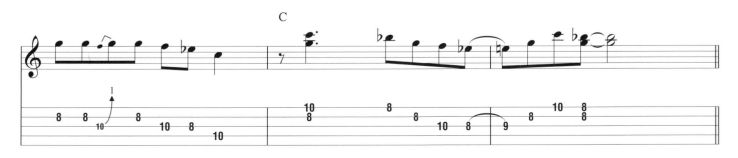

THE "MY BABE" RHYTHM LICK

"Good Mornin' Blues," below, shows how to play a blues rhythm lick for backup that has been used in many well-known blues, R&B, and rock tunes like "My Babe" (Little Walter), "Can I Get a Witness" (Marvin Gaye and the Rolling Stones), "(Goin' to) Kansas City" (the Beatles' version), "Bread and Butter" (the Newbeats), and "You Turn Me On" (Ian Whitcomb)… just to name a few!

Once again, you can see how many urban, pop, and R&B licks grew out of older acoustic blues styles. Like Muddy Waters, Little Walter was a Southern bluesman who grew up hearing and playing acoustic blues. When he, Muddy, and other acoustic blues players moved to Chicago, they "went electric" and added drums and full bands to modernize their sound. But, they played basically the same licks they had played "down South," only their instrument (guitar or harp) was amplified. Many of their signature riffs and licks were used later in pop, rock, and soul music.

The "My Babe" lick can be based on the F formation or the barre, and can have a few different rhythmic feels:

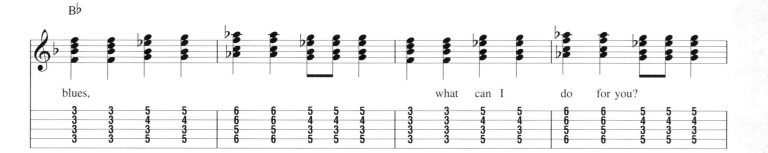

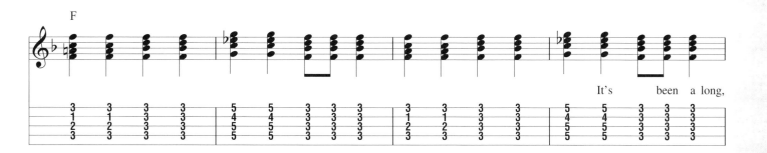

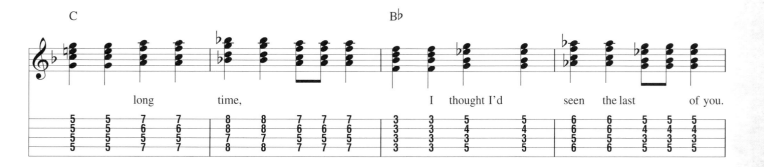

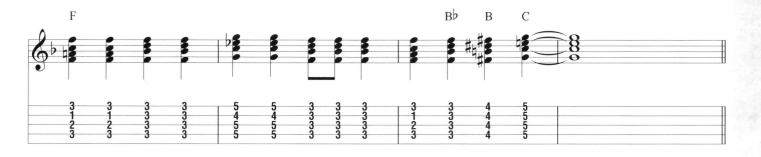

PLAYING THE BLUES IN C TUNING

In the 19th century, classical banjo players used C tuning, and instruction manuals offered it as the only correct tuning. Later, during the folk music era of the late 1950s through the early 1960s, it was the favorite tuning of Pete Seeger and other urban folkies. It has also been popular among old time players like Dock Boggs, Buell Kazee, and Hobart Smith. Earl Scruggs and other early bluegrassers sometimes played in C tuning, as well.

C tuning is the same as G tuning, except the fourth string is tuned down to C, instead of D. The C tuning chords duplicate the G tuning chords, except you have to compensate for the low-tuned fourth string. Two benefits of this tuning are the low C bass note (the open fourth string) with the first position C chord, and the easier-to-play F chord:

CHORDS IN C TUNING

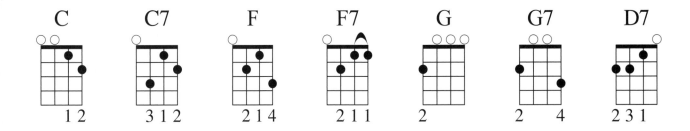

MONOTONE THUMB BASS

The monotone thumb bass, one of the main guitar fingerpicking blues techniques, is easily adapted to the C-tuned banjo. In this style of fingerpicking, your thumb plays a constant, four-beats-to-the-bar bass note on a low string, often the root note of the chord being played. At the same time, you pick the melody with your fingers. If you're singing and playing accompaniment, the thumb continues to play four bass notes to the bar, and the fingers brush up on the treble strings to fill out the rhythms as needed. Those brushes could come during "holes" in the vocal line, or you could play a steady pattern, like these two:

MONOTONE THUMB BASS PATTERNS

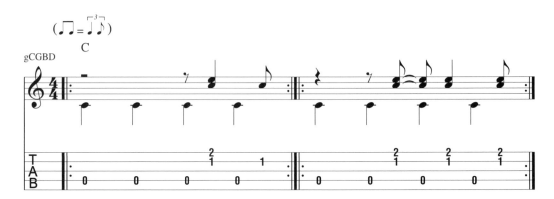

Lightnin' Hopkins was a very widely imitated Texas blues guitarist. His 1950s recordings inspired many blues and early rock (rockabilly) players. He, and other Texas blues guitarists like Mance Lipscomb, played monotone thumb bass. So did Big Bill Broonzy (in songs like "Hey Hey Hey," covered later by Eric Clapton), Robert Johnson, and other Mississippi players. Lightnin's "Baby Please Don't Go" is a classic example of the style, and listen to Lipscomb's "Come Back Baby."

The following arrangement of the old blues tune "See See Rider" features monotone thumb bass picking. The arrangement is reminiscent of Mance Lipscomb's style of picking.

"SEE SEE RIDER"

Here's another blues standard, rendered in the monotone thumb bass style. This version of "Stealin'" is roughly based on the 1928 Memphis Jug Band recording.

"STEALIN'" (SOLO)

ALTERNATING THUMB BASS

The other most popular blues guitar fingerpicking style features an alternating thumb bass. Sometimes called "raggy blues," or "ragtime blues," this technique is often associated with the "Piedmont school" of acoustic blues players, from the Southern states on or near the East Coast. Reverend Gary Davis, Blind Blake, Blind Boy Fuller, Elizabeth Cotten, Blind Willie McTell, and Brownie McGhee are often linked with the Piedmont style. But so is Mississippi John Hurt! All these fingerpickers had a big influence on the 1960s folksinger/songwriters like Bob Dylan, Dave Van Ronk, and Paul Simon. The raggy blues style is also heard in classic rock tunes like "Dust in the Wind."

This picking style is readily adaptable to the C-tuned banjo, with its low fourth string/bass note. Raggy blues pickers play alternating bass notes with their thumb, while picking melody with their fingers. The bass notes are usually the root and fifth, but they can be any notes in the chord being played.

The next two popular blues tunes illustrate this picking style. "The Midnight Special" is associated with Lead Belly (Huddie Ledbetter), the great 12-string guitarist/singer/songwriter who became famous in the 1940s. In addition to this tune, he wrote or popularized "In the Pines," "Goodnight Irene," "The Rock Island Line," "Cotton Fields," "Gallows Pole," and other tunes that have crossed over and become rock or pop standards. "Careless Love" has been recorded by too many blues artists to list. Both songs are arranged a la Mississippi John Hurt, a blues guitarist who greatly influenced the 1960s generation of fingerpicking folksingers.

"THE MIDNIGHT SPECIAL" (SOLO)

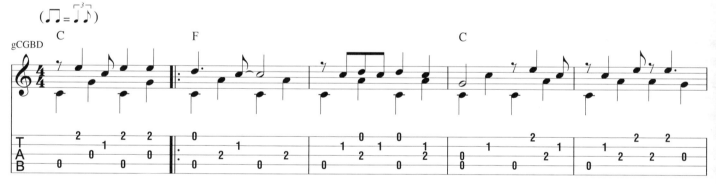

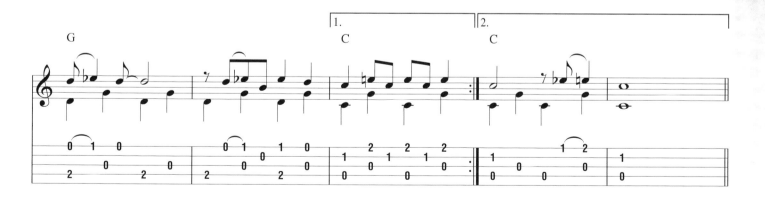

"CARELESS LOVE" (SOLO)

BLUES WITH RAGTIME CHORD CHANGES

Some popular blues tunes from the 1920s and 1930s have ragtime or Tin Pan Alley chord changes. They're a far cry from the three-chord, 12-bar blues. "Nobody Knows You When You're Down and Out," popularized by the "Empress of the Blues," Bessie Smith, is one of many such tunes that has endured and is still performed and recorded today by many artists. Eric Clapton included it in his eight-Grammy-winning *Unplugged* album.

Here are the chord shapes for this tune, arranged below in the monotone thumb bass style:

RAGTIME CHORDS IN C TUNING

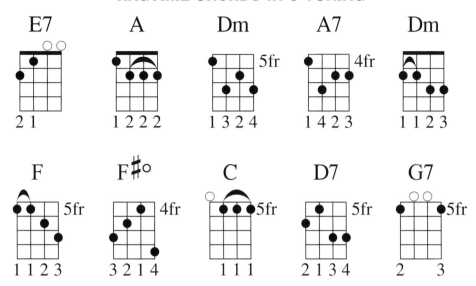

"NOBODY KNOWS YOU WHEN YOU'RE DOWN AND OUT" (SOLO)

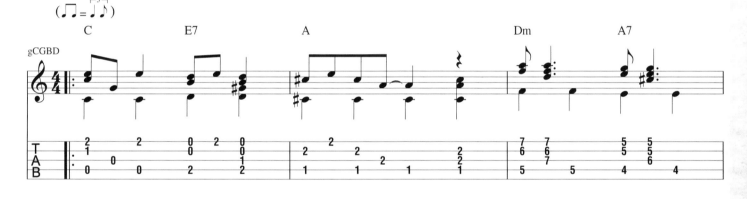

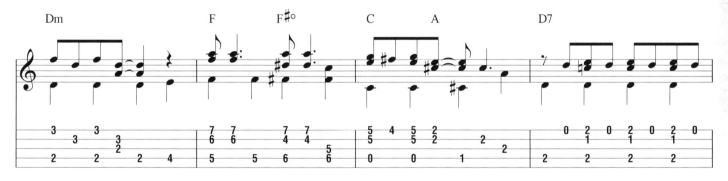

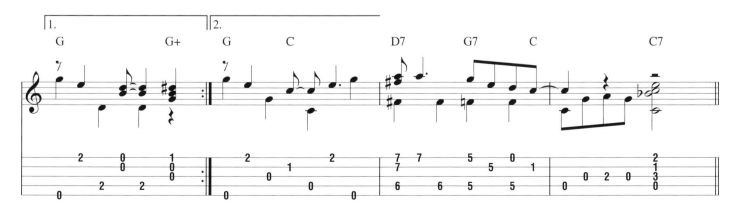

IMPROVISING WITH THE C MINOR PENTATONIC SCALE

Earlier in the book, the solos for "Fourteen Years" and "So Long" are based on the G minor pentatonic scale. You can use the C minor pentatonic scale, below, to play blues melodies or ad lib blues solos in the key of C.

Repeat over and over, as written:

C MINOR PENTATONIC SCALE (FIRST POSITION)

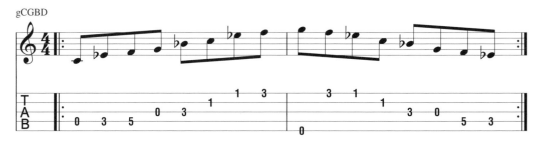

Here's another verse of "So Long," in the key of C. The first time around, the banjo plays *fills*—brief, improvised musical phrases that fill the pauses in the vocal line. During the singing, the banjo employs the monotone bass backup style, but strums chords rather than a single bass note. The second 12-bar features an ad lib-style solo. The fills and the solo are based partly on the C minor pentatonic, and partly on the chords. *You play the chord changes and make up licks from the notes in the chords, augmented by notes from the minor pentatonic scale.*

"SO LONG" (KEY OF C, BACKUP AND SOLO)

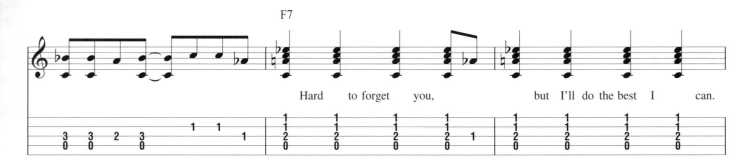

PLAYING THE BLUES IN E
(G TUNING WITH RE-TUNED FIFTH STRING)

E has long been a favored key for blues guitar players. Many famous pickers played almost exclusively in E, including Jimmy Reed, Lightnin' Hopkins, Guitar Slim, Muddy Waters (when he played electric guitar), and Big Boy Arthur Crudup… just to name a few. They often used a capo when a higher key suited their voice, so that they could play their favorite E licks in other keys. The key-of-E licks these players popularized became staples in early rockabilly and rock music. Listen to Lightnin' Hopkins play the blues, then hear the guitar playing in the original "Susie-Q" (by Dale Hawkins with James Burton on guitar), Buddy Holly's "That'll Be the Day" solo, or Elvis Presley's "Little Sister," featuring Hank Garland on the 6-string.

When playing banjo in the key of E, tune your fifth string up to G♯ or B. Even though the high string is rarely played in the key-of-E arrangements that follow, it rings out audibly when you play energetically.

To get used to the key-of-E chords pictured below, play "Didn't See It Comin'." It resembles some of Blind Willie McTell's 8-bar blues tunes.

CHORDS IN E

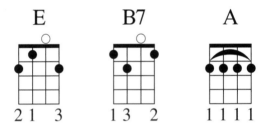

Notice that the thumb often brushes down and plays two low notes at once in the monotone, four-beats-to-the-bar thumb-bass accompaniment.

"DIDN'T SEE IT COMIN'" (BACKUP AND SOLO)

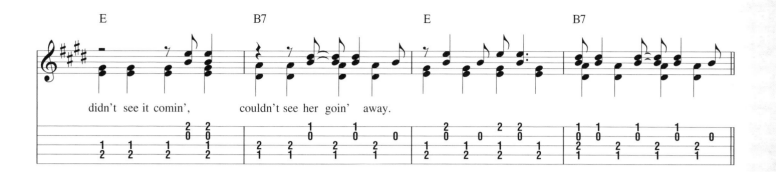

didn't see it comin', couldn't see her goin' away.

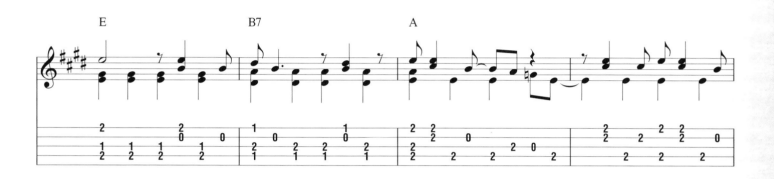

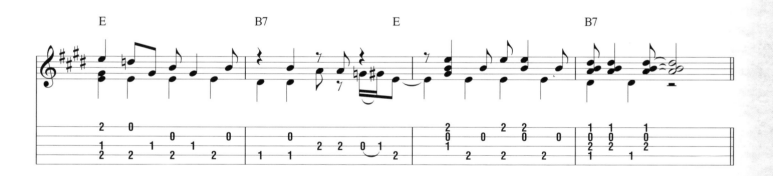

Many classic "E licks" are demonstrated in the following version of the old blues, "Betty and Dupree." It's played in Lightnin' Hopkins' style, with a monotone thumb/bass. Notice the third string hammer-ons, which are one of the reasons E is such a good blues key. The open third string turns the E chord into E minor. *The blues is not exactly major or minor, but sits on the fence and includes minor and major notes, so this single hammer-on is a primeval blues lick.* Two other fundamental key-of-E blues moves are: the slide up on the second and third strings, found in the third bar of "Betty and Dupree," and the "choking third string lick" that's played at the end of that bar and elsewhere in the tune.

The "Shuffle Blues" that follows shows how to build a solo out of up-the-neck chords in the key of E. Here are the chord shapes used in this 12-bar blues:

UP-THE-NECK CHORDS IN E

SHUFFLE BLUES (IN E)

PLAYING THE BLUES IN D TUNING

In D tuning, the open banjo strings make a D major chord: f♯, D, F♯, A, D. Old-time pickers often tune this way, and early bluegrassers used it as well (listen to Earl Scruggs' "Reuben's Train" and "John Henry"; Ralph Stanley's "Hard Times" and Don Reno's "Home Sweet Home"). The first three-finger style tune that a very young Earl Scruggs worked out was "Reuben's Train" in D tuning. Discounting the high F♯/fifth string, D tuning is the same as the top four strings of a very popular open D guitar tuning, used by blues players like Elmore James, Willie McTell, and Blind Willie Johnson, just to name a few.

D tuning chords are just like G tuning chords "moved up a string." For example, compare the G7 in G tuning to the D7 in D tuning:

CHORD COMPARISON

G7

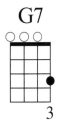

3

D7

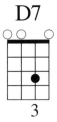

3

Here are some more D tuning chord shapes:

CHORDS IN D TUNING

G

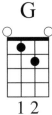

1 2

A7

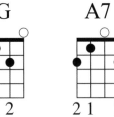

2 1 3

A

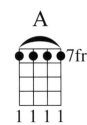

7fr

1 1 1 1

D7

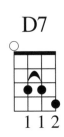

1 1 2

The following version of the old gospel tune, "This Train," is in the alternating thumb style of Willie McTell. It has a flavor similar to his open-D arrangement of "Statesboro Blues." It also resembles Doc Watson's fingerpicking on the blues standard, "Sitting on Top of the World." Sometimes, the thumb reaches up to the fifth string, creating a double-alternating pattern (fourth string/third string/fifth string/third string), but all the melody notes are played with the fingers on the first and second strings. The high D chord on the 7th and 9th frets (at the fifth bar and throughout the tune), and the barred A at the 7th fret, are characteristic D tuning blues licks.

"THIS TRAIN" (SOLO)

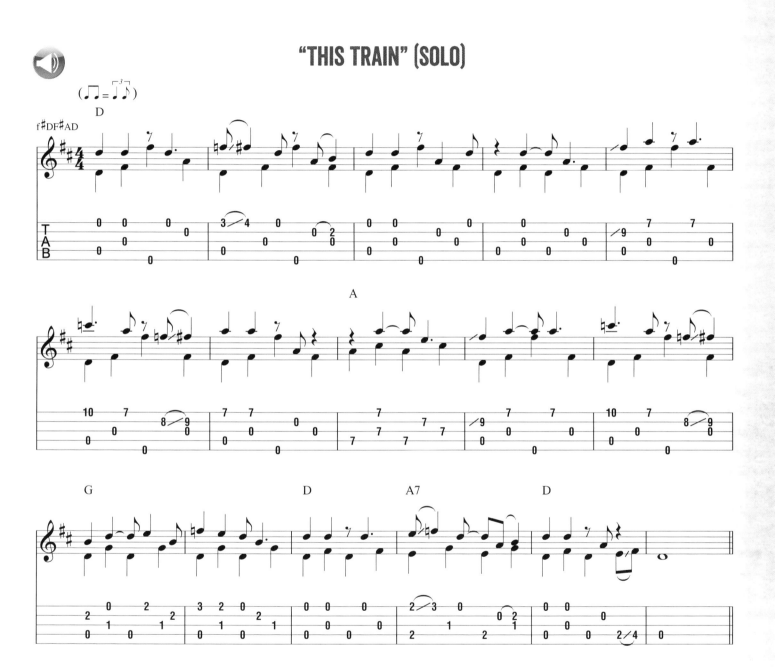

Blind Willie Johnson also played in the alternating thumb bass style, using a slide and usually playing one-chord songs, like the old folk tune "John Henry." Many bottleneck players used this one-chord approach and played most of the melody on the first string. For examples of this style, listen to Blind Willie Johnson's "Motherless Children" and "Keep Your Lamp Trimmed and Burning." The octave licks, played on the first and fourth strings, resemble Skip James' playing on "I'm So Glad." The tune is played twice on the accompanying audio track, and the second time, a slide is used.

"JOHN HENRY" (TWO SOLO VERSIONS)

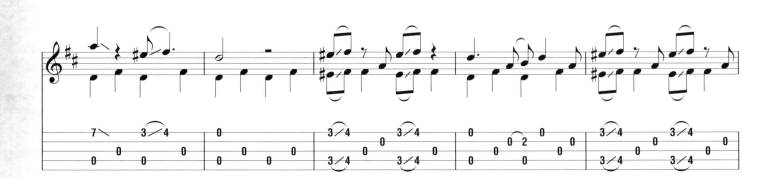

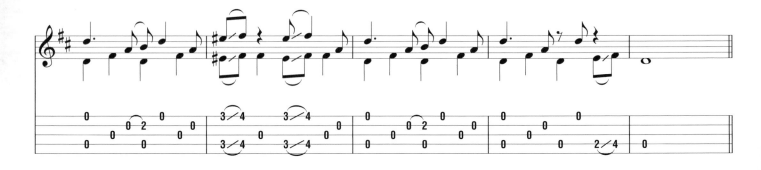

Skip James, a Mississippi blues man who influenced many blues and rock players, tuned his guitar to Dm. This duplicates the banjo's D tuning except that the third string is tuned down to F instead of F♯. You can approximate James's moody, unique blues sound in standard D tuning, as shown in "Worried Blues," below. The ad lib, between-the-vocal licks are based mostly on this D minor pentatonic scale:

D MINOR PENTATONIC SCALE (FIRST POSITION)

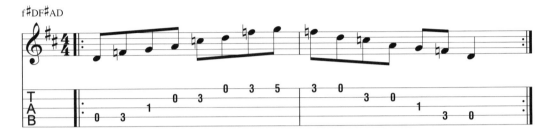

The song begins and ends with Skip James-style turnarounds. Here are some more variations:

TURNAROUNDS IN D

The fills that occur in between vocal phrases in "Worried Blues" are typical of Skip James's D tuning style (bars 5–6, 9–10, and 13–14).

"WORRIED BLUES"

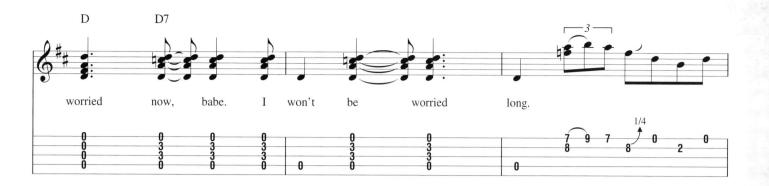

worried   now,   babe.   I   won't   be   worried   long.

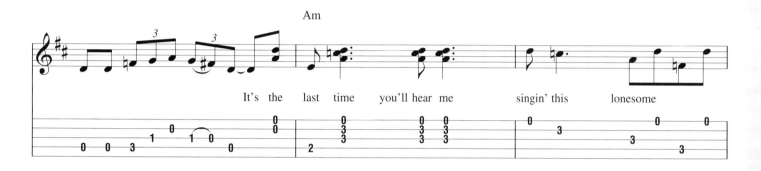

It's the   last   time   you'll hear me   singin' this   lonesome

song.

THE SONGS

The exercises throughout this book offer only one or two verses of each song. Here are some more complete versions for your enjoyment, with a few timeless blues classics thrown in for good measure. You can sing the tunes reading the lyric sheets, and strum or pick accompaniment via the corresponding chord letter names. Additionally, songs that weren't included in the previous text now include written and recorded instrumental solos, featured at the start of the audio tracks, where applicable. When you sing the tunes, you can play an occasional solo between verses, or play a solo at the beginning or end of the tune.

"AIN'T NOBODY'S BUSINESS"

This jazzy 8-bar blues was recorded by Bessie Smith, Alberta Hunter, and other blues singers in the 1920s. Billie Holiday's uptempo swing version was one of countless jazz and blues interpretations, and in 1949, Jimmy Witherspoon's slow, soulful version made #1 on the R&B Records charts. Contemporary artists like Susan Tedeschi, Willie Nelson, Eric Clapton, and Taj Mahal continue to keep this classic alive. Note the Tin Pan Alley-style introductory verse.

G tuning: gDGBD

Intro:

C   E7   Am   E7 A7   Dm A7
There is nothin' I can do or nothin' I can say, that folks won't criticize me.

Dm   A7   D7   G♯7   G7
So I'm goin' to do just what I want to anyway. I don't care if they all despise me.

Verse:

C   E7   F   F♯°
1. If I should take a notion to jump into the ocean,

C   A7   D7   G7   C A7 D7 G7
It ain't nobody's business what I do, do, do, do.

C   E7   F   F♯°
If me and my baby fuss and fight, and the next minute, we're all right,

C   A7   D7   G7   C C7 F Fm C G7
It ain't nobody's business what we do.

Additional verses, same chord progression:

2. I'm three times seven, and that makes twenty-one,

   So it ain't nobody's business what I do, do, do, do.

   If I go to church on Sunday and cabaret all night Monday,

   It ain't nobody's business what I do.

3. If my friend runs out of money and I say "Take all mine, honey,"

    It ain't nobody's business what I do, do, do, do.

    If I give her my last nickel and it leaves me in a pickle,

    It ain't nobody's business what I do.

4. If one night we have ham and bacon, and the next night, ain't nothin' shakin',

    It ain't nobody's business what we do, do, do, do.

    Oh Lord, Lord, Lord, oh Lord, Lord, Lord,

    It ain't nobody's business what I do.

"CARELESS LOVE"

Buddy Bolden, one of the originators of jazz, made this tune famous around 1900, and it has been recorded by blues, jazz, country, rock, bluegrass, and folk singers ever since. It's the lament of a girl whose man left her after getting her pregnant. Listen to the solo on the earlier "Careless Love" track and read it on page 28.

C tuning: gCGBD

    C   G   C   G
1. Love, oh love, oh careless love. Love, oh love, oh careless love.

    C   F   C   G   C
    Love, oh love, oh, careless love, you see what love has done to me.

    C   G   C   G
2. When I wore my apron low, when I wore my apron low,

    C   F   C   G   C
    When I wore my apron low, you followed me through ice and snow.

    C   G   C   G
3. Now my apron strings won't pin. Now my apron strings won't pin.

    C   F   C   G   C
    Now my apron strings won't pin. You pass my door and won't come in.

    C   G   C   G
4. I cried last night and the night before. I cried last night and the night before.

    C   F   C   G   C
    I cried last night and the night before. Gonna cry tonight and cry no more.

"DIDN'T SEE IT COMIN'"

I wrote this tune in a format similar to Blind Willie McTell's "Searching the Desert for the Blues." There are many 8-bar blues tunes that have a similar progression and melody, but different lyrics. Listen to the solo and vocal on the earlier "Didn't See It Comin'" track and read it on page 32.

G tuning with the fifth string tuned up to B: bDGBD

   E   B7   A
1.   I was blind, I was sleepin', I was walkin' around in a daze.

     E   B7   E
    I didn't see it comin', couldn't see her goin' away.

  B7   E   B7   A
2.   Though she would go out in the evening, stay out 'til the break of day,

     E   B7   E
    I didn't see it comin', couldn't see her goin' away.

  B7   E   B7   A
3.   Although she spent all my money, spent all the money I hadn't even made,

     E   B7   E
    I didn't see it comin', couldn't see her goin' away.

  B7   E   B7   A
4.   I bought her ticket at the station, packed her suitcase, what can I say?

     E   B7   E
    I didn't see it comin', couldn't see her goin' away.

"FOURTEEN YEARS"

Like "Walking Blues" and many other 12-bar Delta blues songs, "Fourteen Years" has the form of a "work song." To achieve a manageable rhythm to their labor, men swinging sledge hammers to break rocks or line track would sing while working. The songs they sang needed to have a pause in the lyric at regular intervals, during which the hammer would come down: "Fourteen years is such a (whap!) long, long time, and when you (whap!) love somebody you just don't (whap!) stop on a dime." Early songs of this type described the work, the captain, or the troubles of the singer, but many blues performers retained the format and sang about their woman instead. I composed this tune for inclusion in an album by the Goin' South Band. Listen to the solo and vocal on the earlier "Fourteen Years" tracks (both versions) and read them on pages 10 and 12.

G tuning: gDGBD

G7
1. Fourteen years is such a long, long time, and if you

G7
Love somebody, you just don't stop on a dime.

G7   **C7**   **G7**
When you love somebody, you just don't stop on a dime.

D7   **C7**   **G**
Fourteen years, fourteen years is such a long, long time.

G7
2. Only thing I ever did that was wrong,

G7
You know I kept on tryin' and tryin' for much too long.

G7   **C7**   **G7**
When you love somebody, you just don't stop on a dime.

D7   **C7**   **G**
Fourteen years is such a long, long time.

G7

3. They'll tell you their new man, he's never the reason why,

G7

But when it all comes down, she'll wind up with that guy.

G7   **C7**   **G7**

When you love somebody, you just don't stop on a dime.

D7   **C7**   **G**

Fourteen years is such a long, long time.

G7

4. May take a year, then again it may take five,

G7

But someday I'll get outta these doggone blues alive.

G7   **C7**   **G7**

When you love somebody, you just don't stop on a dime.

D7   **C7**   **G**

Fourteen years is such a long, long time.

"FRANKIE AND JOHNNY"

In 1899, Frankie Baker caught her beau, Allen Britt (also called Albert), with another woman and shot and killed him. Bill Dooley wrote a song about the incident, and as the recorded versions of the ballad multiplied, the couple morphed into Frankie and Johnny. Their song fueled several movies, plays, a ballet, and recorded performances by (among others) Lead Belly, Johnny Cash, Sam Cooke, Lonnie Donegan, Bob Dylan, Mississippi John Hurt, Charlie Patton, Charlie Poole, Jerry Lee Lewis, Elvis Presley, Jimmie Rodgers, Gene Vincent, Fats Waller, Van Morrison, Stevie Wonder, Louis Armstrong, Count Basie, Dave Brubeck, Duke Ellington, and Benny Goodman. The following version combines elements of Big Bill Broonzy and Furry Lewis's recordings.

G tuning: gDGBD

    G   **G7**

1. Frankie and Johnny were sweethearts. Oh Lordy, how they could love.

    C   **G**

    Swore to be true to each other, just as true as the stars above.

                A   **D7**   **G**   **D7**

    He was her man, but he done her wrong.

    G   **G7**

2. Frankie went down to the corner, to buy a bucket of beer.

    C   **G**

    She said, "Mister bartender, has my lovin' Johnny been here?

                A   **D7**   **G**   **D7**

    He's my man, he wouldn't do me no wrong."

Additional verses, same chord progression:

3. "I don't want to cause you no trouble, I ain't gonna tell you no lie.

    I saw Johnny an hour ago with a girl named Nellie Blye.

    He was your man, but he's doin' you wrong."

4. Frankie went down to the hotel. Didn't go there for fun.

    Underneath her kimono, she carried a forty-four gun.

    He was her man, but he was doin' her wrong.

5. Frankie looked over the transom. She saw, to her surprise,

    There on a sofa sat Johnny, makin' love to Nellie Blye.

    He was her man, but he was doin' her wrong.

6. Frankie threw back her kimono, took out her old forty-four.

    Rooty-toot-toot, three times she shot right through that hardwood door.

    Shot her man, he was doin' her wrong.

7. "Bring out the rubber-tired hearses, bring out the rubber-tired hacks.

    They're takin' my Johnny to the graveyard, but they ain't gonna bring him back.

    He was my man, and he done me wrong."

8. "Bring out a thousand policemen, to carry me away.

Lock me down in a dungeon cell and throw that key away.

I shot my man, he was doin' me wrong."

9. Frankie she said to the warden, "What do you reckon they'll do?"

The warden, he said to Frankie, "It's the electric chair for you,

'Cause you shot your man, he was doin' you wrong."

10. This story has no moral; this story has no end.

This story only just goes to show that there ain't no good in men.

He was her man, and he done her wrong.

"JOHN HENRY"

This folk song, around a century old, celebrates a workingman who refused to be replaced by a machine. John Henry beat the steam drill, but died trying. Blues singers like Brownie McGhee, Lead Belly, and Josh White have kept the legend alive, as have bluegrass and country singers, and rockers like Van Morrison and Bruce Springsteen. Listen to the solo on the earlier "John Henry" track and read it on page 38.

D tuning: f♯DF♯AD

D

1. When John Henry he was a little baby boy, sittin' on his papa's knee,

    Well, he picked up a hammer and a little piece of steel, said,

    "Hammer's gonna be the death of me, Lord, Lord, hammer's gonna be the death of me."

D

2. Well, the captain he said to John Henry, "Gonna bring me that steam drill 'round.

    Gonna bring me a steam drill out on the job,

    Gonna whup that steel on down, down, down, gonna whup that steel on down."

Additional verses:

3. John Henry said to his captain, "A man ain't nothin' but a man,

    And before I let that steam drill beat me down,

    I'll die with a hammer in my hand, Lord, Lord, I'll die with a hammer in my hand."

4. John Henry said to his shaker, "Shaker, why don't you pray?

    'Cause if I miss this little piece of steel,

    Tomorrow be your buryin' day, Lord, Lord, tomorrow be your buryin' day."

5. John Henry was drivin' on the mountain and his hammer was flashing fire.

    And the last words I heard that poor boy say,

    "Gimme a cool drink of water 'fore I die, Lord, Lord, gimme a cool drink of water 'fore I die."

6. John Henry he drove fifteen feet, the steam drill only made nine,

    But he hammered so hard that he broke his poor heart,

    And he laid down his hammer and he died, Lord, Lord, he laid down his hammer and he died.

7. They took John Henry to the graveyard and they buried him in the sand.

    And every locomotive comes a-roaring by says,

    "There lies a steel-driving man, Lord, Lord, there lies a steel-driving man."

"THE MIDNIGHT SPECIAL"

Lead Belly popularized this old folk blues, sung by a prisoner about the train that passes his penitentiary at midnight, just like the train in Johnny Cash's "Folsom Prison Blues." The long list of folk, blues, rock, and R&B artists that have recorded it includes many British rockers like Eric Clapton, Paul McCartney, and Spencer Davis (as well as Irishman Van Morrison). They probably first heard it from Lonnie Donegan, who popularized the tune in the UK in 1958. Donegan's "skiffle music" (acoustic folk) hits inspired many Brits to pick up a guitar. Listen to the solo on the earlier "Midnight Special" track and read it on page 27.

C tuning: gCGBD

Verse:

  C   F   C

1. Well, you get up in the morning; hear the work bell ring.

  C   G   C

   You go a-marching to the table; you see the same damn thing.

  C   F   C

   Knife and fork are on the table, nothin' in your pan.

  C   G   C

   But if you say a thing about it, you're in trouble with the man.

Chorus:

  C   F   C

   Let the Midnight Special shine her light on me.

  C   G   C

   Let the Midnight Special shine her ever-lovin' light on me.

Additional verses, same chord progression:

2. Yonder comes Miss Rosie. How in the world did you know?

   By the way she wears her apron and the clothes she wore.

   Umbrella on her shoulder, piece of paper in her hand,

   She come to tell the governor, "Turn loose of my man." (*Chorus*)

3. If you're ever in Houston, well you'd better walk right;

   You'd better not swagger, and you better not fight,

   Or the sheriff will arrest you, he's gonna take you down.

   You can bet your bottom dollar, you're penitentiary bound. (*Chorus*)

"NOBODY KNOWS YOU WHEN YOU'RE DOWN AND OUT"

Jimmy Cox wrote this bluesy ballad during prohibition (hence the "bootleg liquor" reference), and Bessie Smith's 1929 recording made it famous. Countless jazz, blues, pop, and soul singers have recorded it, and during the folk revival of the 1960s it was a part of many a guitarists' repertoire. Eric Clapton included it in his multi-Grammy winning *Unplugged* album, and said it was the first song he dared to sing in public. Listen to the solo on the earlier "Nobody Knows You When You're Down and Out" track and read it on page 29.

C tuning: gCGBD

Intro: D7 G7 C G7

Verse:

    C   E7   A   Dm   A7   Dm

1. Once I lived the life of a millionaire and spent all my money without a care.

    F   F#°   C   A

Takin' my friends out for a mighty fine time,

         D7   G   G+

Buying bootleg liquor, champagne, and wine.

    C   E7   A   Dm   A7   Dm

2. Then I began to fall so low, I didn't have no money and no place to go.

     F   F#°   C   A

If I ever get my hands on a dollar again,

      D7   G   G+

I'm gonna hold on to it 'til the eagle grins, 'cause…

    C E7 A   Dm   A7   Dm

3. Nobody knows you when you're down and out.

    F   F#°   C   A

In your pocket, there's not one penny,

    D7   G   G+

And all your friends, well, you haven't any.

C	E7	A	Dm	A7	Dm

4. Just get back up on your two feet again; everybody wants to be your long lost friend.

F	F#°	C	A

It's mighty strange, but without a doubt,

D7	G	C

Nobody knows you when you're down and out.

D7	G7	C	C7

I mean, when you're down and out.

"SEE SEE RIDER"

Ma Rainey had a hit with this 12-bar blues in 1924, and it has been on the pop or R&B charts in nearly every decade since then. It's sometimes sung "Easy Rider," referring to a back-door man, a woman of easy virtue, or some kind of morally questionable lover! Listen to the solo and vocal on the earlier "See See Rider" track and read it on page 25.

C tuning: gCGBD

C

1. See, See Rider, see what you have done.

F7   **C**

See, See Rider, see what you have done.

C   G7   **F**   **C**

You made me love you, now your man has come.

Additional verses, same chord progression:

2. See, See Rider, where'd you stay last night?

   See, See Rider, where'd you stay last night?

   You come home this morning, the sun was shining bright.

3. I'm goin' away, baby, I won't be back 'til fall.

   I'm goin' away, baby, I won't be back 'til fall.

   If I find me a good gal, I won't be back at all.

"ST. JAMES INFIRMARY BLUES"

This minor-key tune, often played at New Orleans funerals, goes back about 300 years. Louis Armstrong recorded a definitive version in 1928. Like many blues songs, including a variant of "St. James Infirmary" recorded by Blind Willie McTell, the singer leaves funeral instructions to his listeners. Bob Dylan's song, "Blind Willie McTell," has some musical similarity to "St. James Infirmary" and mentions the St. James Hotel.

G tuning with fifth string raised to A: aDGBD

     Am   E7   Am   Dm Am E7

1. I was down in Old Joe's barroom, by the corner of the square.

     Am   E7   Am   F   E7   Am E7

The drinks were served as usual, and the usual crowd was there.

     Am   E7   Am   Dm   Am E7

2. On my left stood Big Joe McKennedy. His eyes were bloodshot red.

      Am   E7   Am   F   E7   Am E7

He took a look at the crowd all around him, and these are the words he said:

     Am E7   Am   Dm Am   E7

3. "I went down to St. James Infirmary. I saw my baby there,

     Am   E7 Am   F   E7   Am E7

She was stretched out on a table, so still, so cold, so fair."

Additional verses, same chord progression:

4. "Let her go, let her go, God bless her, wherever she may be.

She may search this wide world over; she'll never find another man like me."

5. "When I die boys, won't you bury me in my brand new Stetson hat?

Put a twenty dollar gold piece on my watch chain, so the boys'll know I died standing pat."

6. "Give me six crapshooters for my pallbearers, and a chorus girl to sing me a song.

Put a jazz band on my hearse wagon. Just to raise hell as we roll along."

7. "And now that you've heard my story, let's have another round of booze.

And if anyone ever should ask you, I've got the St. James Infirmary blues."

"ST. LOUIS BLUES"

This blues classic was written in 1914 by W. C. Handy, the famous composer, collector, and publisher of blues songs. Countless blues and jazz artists have recorded it, and you can watch and hear Bessie Smith sing it in the 1925 film *St. Louis Blues*. The song begins and ends with the typical 12-bar blues format, with some jazzy chord embellishments. The middle minor-key section is an eight-bar phrase and is often played with a Latin rhythm.

G tuning: gDGBD

Verse:

    C   F7   C   Cmaj7 C7
1. I hate to see that ev'nin' sun go down.

    F7   A♭   G7   C F C
    I hate to see that ev'nin' sun go down,

    G7   C   F C G7
    'Cause that gal of mine, no longer is around.

    C   F7   C Cmaj7 C7
2. Feelin' tomorrow like I feel today,

    F7   A♭   G7   C F C
    Feelin' tomorrow the way I feel today,

      G7   C   F C G7
    I'll pack my trunk, and make my getaway.

Middle Section:

Cm	**Fm6**	**G7 F G° G7**

St. Louis woman with her diamond rings,

Fm6	**G7**	**Cm**	**G7**

Pulls that man 'round by her apron strings.

Cm	**Fm**	**G7 F G° G7**

If it wasn't for powder and her store-bought hair,

Fm6	**G7**	**Cm D7 G7**

That gal of mine wouldn't have gone nowhere, nowhere.

Verse:

C7	**F7**	**C Cmaj7**

3. Got the St. Louis blues, I'm as blue as a man can be.

F7	**C F C**

That woman got a heart like a rock cast in the sea,

G7	**C F C C7**

Or else she wouldn't have gone so far from me.

etc.
(to vocal)

I hate to see...

"STAGOLEE"

Here's another murder, immortalized in song. In 1895, a St. Louis pimp named Lee Sheldon (nicknamed Stag Lee) got into a drunken barroom argument with his friend, William Lyons. Lyons grabbed Sheldon's hat, and Sheldon drew a revolver and shot and killed Lyons. In the many variations of the tune written about the incident, the killer became Stagolee, Stackerlee, or Stagger Lee. Blues, rock, R&B, jazz, folk, and country performers have had hits singing about him. Several movie soundtracks, including *Porky's Revenge*, *Black Snake Moan*, and *Grindhouse* have featured some version of the tune. The arrangement below is based roughly on Mississippi John Hurt's recording.

D tuning: f♯DF♯AD

D
1. Stagolee was a bad man, everybody knows.

G   **D**
Paid one hundred dollars just to buy him a suit of clothes.

        A   **D**
He's a bad man, that cruel Stagolee.

D
2. Billy DeLyons told Stagolee, "Please don't take my life.

G   **D**
I got two little babes at home and a darlin', lovin' wife."

        A   **D**
He's a bad man, that cruel Stagolee.

Additional verses, same chord progression:

3. "What do I care 'bout your two little babes, what do I care 'bout your wife?

    You done stole my Stetson hat and I'm bound to take your life."

    He's a bad man, that cruel Stagolee.

4. Stagolee, cruel Stagolee, pulled out a forty-four.

    When I spied poor Billy DeLyons, he was lyin' dead on the floor.

    He's a bad man, that cruel Stagolee.

5. Gentlemen of the jury, what do you think of that?

   Stagolee killed Billy DeLyons 'bout a five-dollar Stetson hat.

   He's a bad man, that cruel Stagolee.

6. Standin' on the gallows, Stagolee did curse.

   The judge said "Let's kill him now, before he kills one of us."

   He's a bad man, that cruel Stagolee.

7. Standin' on the gallows, with his head held high,

   At twelve o'clock they killed him, they were all glad to see him die.

   He's a bad man, that cruel Stagolee.

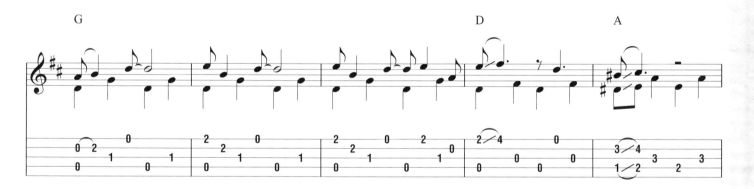

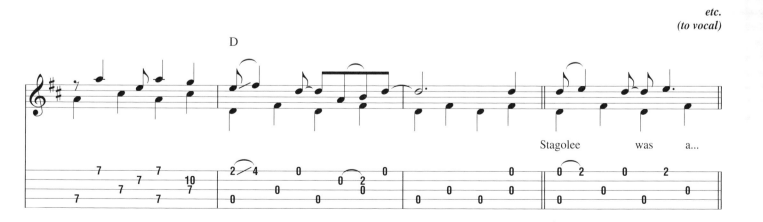

"STEALIN'"

This bluesy ballad was sung by the Memphis Jug Band and other Southern jug bands of the 1920s. It was revived by folksingers of the 1960s. Listen to the solo on the earlier "Stealin'" track and read it on page 26.

C tuning: gCGBD

Intro: G7

Verse:

    C   C7
1. Put your arms around me like a circle 'round the sun.

     F

I wanna love you, mama, like my easy rider done.

Chorus:

    F   C G C   F   C G C
You don't believe I love you, look what a fool I've been.

    C   G C   F   C G C
You don't believe I'm sinkin', look what a hole I'm in.

    C   C7   F   Fm
Stealin', stealin', pretty mama don't-cha tell on me.

      C   G   C G7
I'm stealin' back to my same old used-to-be.

Additional verse, same chord progression:

2. The woman I love, she's my height and size.

     She's a married woman, comes to see me sometimes. (*Chorus*)

"THIS TRAIN"

Many blues singers/guitarists have included traditional gospel songs in their repertoire. Some, like Blind Willie Johnson, sang gospel exclusively. The old gospel tune "This Train" became a hit for Sister Rosetta Tharpe, a very bluesy guitarist and singer, in the 1930s, and countless singers of many musical genres have since recorded it. The song inspired Woody Guthrie's autobiography, *Bound for Glory*, as well as the movie that was based on Woody's book. Listen to the solo on the earlier "This Train" track and read it on page 37.

D tuning: f♯DF♯AD

    D
1. This train is bound for glory, this train.

    D   **A**
    This train is bound for glory, this train.

    D   **G**
    This train is bound for glory. Don't carry nothing but the righteous and the holy.

    D   **A7**   **D**
    This train is bound for glory, this train.

    D
2. This train don't carry no gamblers, this train.

    D   **A**
    This train don't carry no gamblers, this train.

    D   **G**
    This train don't carry no gamblers, no hypocrites, no midnight ramblers,

    D   **A7**   **D**
    This train is bound for glory, this train.

Additional verses, same chord progression:

3. This train is built for speed now, this train.

    This train is built for speed now, this train.

    This train is built for speed now, fastest train you ever did see,

    This train is bound for glory, this train.

4. This train don't carry no liars, this train.

    This train don't carry no liars, this train.

    This train don't carry no liars, no hypocrites, and no high fliers,

    This train is bound for glory, this train.

5. This train don't carry no rustlers, this train.

    This train don't carry no rustlers, this train.

    This train don't carry no rustlers, side street walkers, two-bit hustlers,

    This train is bound for glory, this train.

USING A CAPO TO PLAY IN OTHER KEYS

So far, you've played the blues in G, C, E, and D, using three different tunings—five, if you count the tuned-up-to-B fifth string for playing in the key of E, and the tuned-up-to-A fifth string for the key of Am. Using a capo, you can use all these tunings, and the techniques that go with them, to play in many different keys. The capo charts below will help you make the adjustments. But first, here are some general capo facts:

- The fifth string must be re-tuned to match the capo. If you capo up two frets, tune the fifth string two frets higher than usual.

- Pretend the capo is the nut and play as you normally would. For example, in G tuning, with the capo on the 2nd fret and the fifth string tuned up two frets higher than usual (to A), the strummed open chord is now an A instead of a G. A C chord is now a D, but it's still the four chord, as it was without a capo. All your G licks and chord shapes can be duplicated, only now they are A licks, and all the chords' names are "two frets higher." The D7 shape is an E7; the F shape is G, and so on.

G TUNING CAPO CHART

Play the shapes of the G chord family

Capo	Key	fifth string
1st fret	A♭	up to A♭
2nd fret	A	up to A
3rd fret	B♭	up to B♭
4th fret	B	up to B
5th fret	C	up to C

G TUNING CAPO CHART, PLAYING IN THE KEY OF E

Play the shapes of the E chord family

Capo	Key	fifth string
1st fret	F	up to A or C
2nd fret	G♭	up to B♭
3rd fret	G	up to B
4th fret	A♭	up to C
5th fret	A	up to C♯

C TUNING CAPO CHART

Play the shapes of the C chord family

Capo	Key	fifth string
1st fret	D♭	up to A♭
2nd fret	D	up to A
3rd fret	E♭	up to B♭
4th fret	E	up to B
5th fret	F	up to C

D TUNING CAPO CHART

Play the shapes of the D chord family

Capo	Key	fifth string
1st fret	E♭	up to G or up to B♭
2nd fret	E	up to G♯ or up to B
3rd fret	F	up to A or up to C
4th fret	G♭	up to B♭
5th fret	G	up to B

LISTENING SUGGESTIONS

Besides listening to the few recorded banjo players who played blues in the past, Papa Charlie Jackson and Gus Cannon, listen to blues guitarists.

Monotone Thumb Players
Some blues guitarists who often used this approach include Robert Johnson, Big Bill Broonzy, Mance Lipscomb, Lightnin' Hopkins, and Brownie McGhee.

Alternating Thumb Players
Listen to Mississippi John Hurt, Reverend Gary Davis, Blind Willie Johnson, Blind Willie McTell, and Blind Blake, just to name a few.

G Tuning Players
Guitarists who often used G tuning include Son House, Fred McDowell, Robert Johnson (capoed up two or three frets), and Muddy Waters (his early acoustic recordings).

D Tuning Players
Skip James used D minor, but his sounds can be duplicated with D tuning. Also listen to Tampa Red, Willie McTell, Blind Willie Johnson, and Elmore James.

Key-of-E Players
Guitarists who usually played in the key of E (often with a capo) include Jimmy Reed, Muddy Waters (the electric slide tunes), Guitar Slim, Lightnin' Hopkins, and Big Boy Arthur Crudup.

Single-String, Up-the-Neck Blues Players
Listen to T-Bone Walker and the three Kings: B.B., Albert, and Freddie, as well as Buddy Guy, Otis Rush, Magic Sam, Eric Clapton, and Stevie Ray Vaughan.

Chuck Berry-Style Double-Note Style
Listen to Chuck!

ABOUT THE AUTHOR

Fred Sokolow is best known as the author of over 150 instructional and transcription books and DVDs for guitar, banjo, Dobro, mandolin, and ukulele. Fred has long been a well-known West Coast multi-string performer and recording artist, particularly on the acoustic music scene. The diverse musical genres covered in his books and DVDs, along with several bluegrass, jazz, and rock CDs he has released, demonstrate his mastery of many musical styles. Whether he's playing Delta bottleneck blues, bluegrass, or old-time banjo, '30s swing guitar or screaming rock solos, he does it with authenticity and passion.

Fred's other banjo books include:

- *Fretboard Roadmaps • 5-String Banjo,* book/CD, Hal Leonard
- *Complete Bluegrass Banjo,* book/CD, Hal Leonard
- *Beatles for Banjo,* book/CD, Hal Leonard
- *101 Tips for 5-String Banjo,* book/CD, Hal Leonard
- *Instant 5-String Banjo,* book, Music Sales America

Email Fred with any questions about this or his other banjo books at: Sokolowmusic.com.